I0187655

Doggy Diary

- Behaviour Edition -

Doggy Diary

- Behaviour Edition -

Unlock the secrets to your dog's bad behaviour.

Scott Corcoran

SK9 GROUP
PTY LTD

Author: Scott Corcoran.
Manager: Scott Corcoran.
Publisher: SK9 Group Pty Ltd.

Copyright

Copyright © 2025 SK9 Group Pty Ltd.
All rights reserved.

No part of this book may be used or reproduced by any means, graphic, electronic, or mechanical, including photocopying, recording, taping, or by any information storage retrieval system without the written permission of the publisher except in the case of brief quotations embodied in critical articles and reviews.

Disclaimer

While the author has made every effort to ensure that the material in this publication is accurate and up to date, you should exercise your own independent skill and judgment before you rely on it. This manual is not a substitute for professional dog training, or independent professional advice. Readers should obtain appropriate professional advice relevant to their dog and particular circumstances.

Neither the publisher, the authors, contributors, or editors assume any liability for any loss resulting from any action taken or reliance made by you on any information or material in this manual (including, without limitation, third party information). You rely on the information within the publication at your own risk and must take your own precautions to ensure the information and advice is current and accurate.

SK9 Group Pty Ltd
Prospect SA 5082
Tel: 0413 067 769
www.adelaidek9.com.au

Contents

LIFE IS

BETTER

WITH A DOG

Dog Information

Insert Photo:

Name:

_____

Breed:

_____

Birthday:

_____

Pedigree No. _____

Microchip No. _____

Registration No. _____

Insurance No. _____

If you find this Diary, please return it to:

Name: _____

Phone: _____

ABC's of Dog Behaviour:

Antecedents trigger behaviour, leading to a consequence which influences future behaviour.

ANTECEDENT

What happens immediately *before*:

- 🐾 Person knocks on front door.

BEHAVIOUR

The observable actions of the dog:

- 🐾 Dog runs to the door and barks.

CONSEQUENCE

What happens immediately *after*:

- 🐾 Person enters and pats dog.

Managing Behaviour:

When it comes to changing your dog's behaviour there are two important concepts:

Firstly you can **manage the environment** to remove the trigger or reduce the intensity of the trigger (Antecedent). This might mean keeping the kitchen counter clear, blocking a window, or using baby gates to limit access.

The next step is to **remove reinforcement** for the behaviour (Consequence). This might mean not giving the dog attention while they are jumping up or resisting the urge to yell at them when they are barking.

Remember, behaviour that is reinforced, even accidentally, will happen more often - and with repetition it will become a habit.

How to Use this Diary:

- Fill out your dog's details, its handy to have these in one place!
- Record anything related to the behaviour you are working on.
- Be fair – note the good *and* the bad.
- Note what happened, before, during and after any behaviour of concern.
- Be precise, describe any triggers or behaviours in detail.
- Be objective – record what you see and hear, without feelings or opinion.
- Describe unknown people or dogs in detail – you are looking for patterns!
- Share your diary with your trainer, behaviour consultant or veterinarian.

PAWSITIVE Vibes

- Enter the **Day, Date** and **Time.**
- Note the weather at the time.
- Note the period – dawn, day, dusk or night.
- Note the temperature.

- Record **Exercise** here.

- Record **Training** here.

- Describe any **Behaviours** here.
- Describe any triggers in as much detail as possible.
- Consider body language before, during and after:
    a. Posture – relaxed or stiff, confident or fearful.
    b. Weight – forward or rearward.
    c. Tail – high, low, or tucked.
    d. Tail movement – stiff, slow, rapid, vibrating.
    e. Ears – relaxed, pinned back, up and forward.
    f. Mouth – relaxed, tongue out, lips curled, snarling.
    g. Bark – note the pitch, length and intensity.
- Look for stress indicators:
    a. Lip licking.
    b. Looking away.
    c. Eye flashing / whale eye.
    d. Piloerection – raised hackles.
- Be objective – only record what you can feel, see, or hear.
- Describe unknown people or dogs in detail – this is super important. You are looking for patterns in behaviour!

M͟ W T F S S   Date: 10͟ / 4͟

Time: 5pm͟   Dawn Day (Dusk) Night   🌡 20͟ º C

Time spent exercising today: ___90 mins___

● Walk ○ Hike ○ Jog / Run ● Fetch ○ Tug ○ Swimming ○ Sport
○ Playing with other dogs ○ Other _____

Notes: Walked to the beach - played fetch with ball.

Time spent training today: ___40 mins___   Rating: ★ ★ ★ ★ ☆

● Walking ○ Sit ○ Down ○ Look ○ Touch ○ Place ● Recall

Repetitions: ___10___   Successful: ___8___

Notes: Practiced recall at the beach.

Behaviours observed today:

Met a few off-leash dogs, played well.

A - On the way back it was dark - passed a large Husky on the other side of the road. Husky barked at him

B - Max stood up on his back legs, lunged, barked, tail was up and stiff, hackles were up. Bark was low pitch, a growl going into a bark.

C - Kept walking past. Tried to get his attention but he wouldn't take a treat.

7

Describe things you like about your dog:

my dog

Describe the behaviour/s that need work:

Enrichment Ideas:

Reduce boredom & stress, and fulfill natural instincts, keeping your dog happy & healthy.

- 🐾 Hide treats in a rolled-up towel.
- 🐾 Scatter treats in the grass.
- 🐾 Freeze a Kong with your dog's favourite treats.

KONG

- 🐾 Try pumpkin or yoghurt on a lick mat.
- 🐾 Cut holes in an empty plastic bottle and fill it with treats - let your dog roll them out.
- 🐾 Fill a kiddie pool with ball pit balls, or empty plastic bottles and hide treats in the pool.
- 🐾 Play fetch, frisbee, tug or flirt pole.
- 🐾 Give your dogs toys names and train them to fetch the right one.

Welcome
we hope you like dogs

Fun Outings For Your Dog:

- Take your dog to the beach, let them dig in the sand and play in the water.
- Take them on a hike in a nearby forest. Take water and treats!
- Go to a dog-friendly Café.
- Take them for a drive and get them a pup cup, or a doggie ice cream.
- Take your dog camping - stay in a tent or dog-friendly cabin.
- Take your dog for a play date with a doggy friend.
- Have a drink at a dog-friendly bar.
- Take them to the pet shop and let them choose a new toy.

M T W T F S S   Date: ___ / ___

Time: _____   Dawn Day Dusk Night   _____ °

Time spent exercising today: _____

○ Walk ○ Hike ○ Jog / Run ○ Fetch ○ Tug ○ Swimming ○ Sport
○ Playing with other dogs ○ Other _____

Notes:

Time spent training today: _____   Rating: ☆ ☆ ☆ ☆ ☆

○ Walking ○ Sit ○ Down ○ Look ○ Touch ○ Place ○ Other

Repetitions: _____   Successful: _____

Notes:

Behaviours observed today (ABC's):

M T W T F S S   Date: ___ / ___

Time: _____   Dawn Day Dusk Night   _____ °

Time spent exercising today: _____

O Walk O Hike O Jog / Run O Fetch O Tug O Swimming O Sport
O Playing with other dogs O Other _____

Notes:

Time spent training today: _____   Rating: ☆ ☆ ☆ ☆ ☆

O Walking O Sit O Down O Look O Touch O Place O Other

Repetitions: _____   Successful: _____

Notes:

Behaviours observed today (ABC's):

M T W T F S S Date: ___ / ___

Time: _____   Dawn Day Dusk Night   _____ °

Time spent exercising today: _____

○ Walk ○ Hike ○ Jog / Run ○ Fetch ○ Tug ○ Swimming ○ Sport
○ Playing with other dogs ○ Other _____

Notes:

Time spent training today: _____   Rating: ✰ ✰ ✰ ✰ ✰

○ Walking ○ Sit ○ Down ○ Look ○ Touch ○ Place ○ Other

Repetitions: _____   Successful: _____

Notes:

Behaviours observed today (ABC's):

M T W T F S S   Date: ___ / ___

Time: _____   Dawn   Day   Dusk   Night   _____ °

Time spent exercising today: _____

○ Walk   ○ Hike   ○ Jog / Run   ○ Fetch   ○ Tug   ○ Swimming   ○ Sport
○ Playing with other dogs   ○ Other _____

Notes:

Time spent training today: _____   Rating: ☆ ☆ ☆ ☆ ☆

○ Walking   ○ Sit   ○ Down   ○ Look   ○ Touch   ○ Place   ○ Other

Repetitions: _____   Successful: _____

Notes:

Behaviours observed today (ABC's):

M T W T F S S   Date: ___ / ___

Time: _____   Dawn Day Dusk Night   _____ °

Time spent exercising today: _____

○ Walk   ○ Hike   ○ Jog / Run   ○ Fetch   ○ Tug   ○ Swimming   ○ Sport
○ Playing with other dogs   ○ Other _____

Notes:

Time spent training today: _____   Rating: ☆ ☆ ☆ ☆ ☆

○ Walking   ○ Sit   ○ Down   ○ Look   ○ Touch   ○ Place   ○ Other

Repetitions: _____   Successful: _____

Notes:

Behaviours observed today (ABC's):

M T W T F S S   Date: ___ / ___

Time: _____   Dawn Day Dusk Night   _____ 0

Time spent exercising today: _____

○ Walk   ○ Hike   ○ Jog / Run   ○ Fetch   ○ Tug   ○ Swimming   ○ Sport
○ Playing with other dogs   ○ Other _____

Notes:

Time spent training today: _____   Rating: ☆ ☆ ☆ ☆ ☆

○ Walking   ○ Sit   ○ Down   ○ Look   ○ Touch   ○ Place   ○ Other

Repetitions: _____   Successful: _____

Notes:

Behaviours observed today (ABC's):

M T W T F S S Date: ___ / ___

Time: _____   Dawn Day Dusk Night   _____ °

Time spent exercising today: _____

○ Walk ○ Hike ○ Jog / Run ○ Fetch ○ Tug ○ Swimming ○ Sport
○ Playing with other dogs ○ Other _____

Notes:

Time spent training today: _____   Rating: ☆ ☆ ☆ ☆ ☆

○ Walking ○ Sit ○ Down ○ Look ○ Touch ○ Place ○ Other

Repetitions: _____   Successful: _____

Notes:

Behaviours observed today (ABC's):

Week One

What went well, and how I can improve: Weekly Rating: ★ ★ ★ ★ ☆

Habit Tracker: Habits (good and bad) that you worked on this week:

Habits	M	T	W	T	F	S	S
	○	○	○	○	○	○	○
	○	○	○	○	○	○	○
	○	○	○	○	○	○	○

Expert Tip #1

Jumping Up

Management

- Don't get overly excited when you get home.

- Reward calm behaviour, and four paws on the floor with affection and treats.

- Ignore the dog: That doesn't mean folding you're arms and becoming a statue. Go about your day until they are calm.

- Control visitors: Ask them not to look at the dog, talk to the dog, or touch the dog until the dog is calm.

- Use a leash or baby gate: Limit access to visitors until the dog settles.

- Reward alternative behaviours: Condition and reinforce an incompatible behaviour like "sit" or "place" for when people arrive.

- Ensure your dog gets enough physical exercise and mental enrichment.

Differential Reinforcement Alternative (DRA) Behaviour

Condition the Clicker, or Marker Word "Yes!".

Condition "Sit" and "Place" cues.

Reward the dog for sitting or remaining on place when visitors arrive.

Practice entering

Tips for Long-Term Success

- Be consistent—every family member and visitor should follow the same rules.

- Avoid yelling or pushing the dog away, as this can be seen as play or attention.

- Consider the "Place" command where the dog goes to a mat when guests arrive.

By understanding the **ABC's of Dog Behaviour** and implementing these strategies, you can teach your dog polite greetings and reduce jumping over time. Patience and consistency are key!

MTWTFSS Date: ___ / ___

Time: _____   Dawn Day Dusk Night   _____ °

Time spent exercising today: _____

○ Walk ○ Hike ○ Jog / Run ○ Fetch ○ Tug ○ Swimming ○ Sport
○ Playing with other dogs ○ Other _____

Notes:

Time spent training today: _____   Rating: ☆ ☆ ☆ ☆ ☆

○ Walking ○ Sit ○ Down ○ Look ○ Touch ○ Place ○ Other

Repetitions: _____   Successful: _____

Notes:

Behaviours observed today (ABC's):

Doggy Diary - Behaviour Edition

M T W T F S S Date: ___ / ___

Time: _____   Dawn Day Dusk Night   _____ °

Time spent exercising today: _____

○ Walk ○ Hike ○ Jog / Run ○ Fetch ○ Tug ○ Swimming ○ Sport
○ Playing with other dogs ○ Other _____

Notes:

Time spent training today: _____   Rating: ☆ ☆ ☆ ☆ ☆

○ Walking ○ Sit ○ Down ○ Look ○ Touch ○ Place ○ Other

Repetitions: _____   Successful: _____

Notes:

Behaviours observed today (ABC's):

M T W T F S S   Date: __ / __

Time: _____   Dawn Day Dusk Night   ____ °

Time spent exercising today: _____

○ Walk   ○ Hike   ○ Jog / Run   ○ Fetch   ○ Tug   ○ Swimming   ○ Sport
○ Playing with other dogs   ○ Other _____

Notes:

Time spent training today: _____   Rating: ☆ ☆ ☆ ☆ ☆

○ Walking   ○ Sit   ○ Down   ○ Look   ○ Touch   ○ Place   ○ Other

Repetitions: _____   Successful: _____

Notes:

Behaviours observed today (ABC's):

M T W T F S S Date: ___ / ___

Time: _____   Dawn Day Dusk Night   _____ °

Time spent exercising today: _____

○ Walk ○ Hike ○ Jog / Run ○ Fetch ○ Tug ○ Swimming ○ Sport
○ Playing with other dogs ○ Other _____

Notes:

Time spent training today: _____   Rating: ☆ ☆ ☆ ☆ ☆

○ Walking ○ Sit ○ Down ○ Look ○ Touch ○ Place ○ Other

Repetitions: _____   Successful: _____

Notes:

Behaviours observed today (ABC's):

M T W T F S S   Date: __ / __

Time: _____   Dawn Day Dusk Night   ____ °

Time spent exercising today: _____

○ Walk ○ Hike ○ Jog / Run ○ Fetch ○ Tug ○ Swimming ○ Sport
○ Playing with other dogs ○ Other _____

Notes:

Time spent training today: _____   Rating: ☆ ☆ ☆ ☆ ☆

○ Walking ○ Sit ○ Down ○ Look ○ Touch ○ Place ○ Other

Repetitions: _____   Successful: _____

Notes:

Behaviours observed today (ABC's):

M T W T F S S Date: ___ / ___

Time: _____   Dawn Day Dusk Night   _____ °

Time spent exercising today: _____

○ Walk ○ Hike ○ Jog / Run ○ Fetch ○ Tug ○ Swimming ○ Sport
○ Playing with other dogs ○ Other _____

Notes:

Time spent training today: _____   Rating: ☆ ☆ ☆ ☆ ☆

○ Walking ○ Sit ○ Down ○ Look ○ Touch ○ Place ○ Other

Repetitions: _____   Successful: _____

Notes:

Behaviours observed today (ABC's):

M T W T F S S   Date: __ / __

Time: _____   Dawn Day Dusk Night   _____ °

Time spent exercising today: _____

○ Walk ○ Hike ○ Jog / Run ○ Fetch ○ Tug ○ Swimming ○ Sport
○ Playing with other dogs ○ Other _____

Notes:

Time spent training today: _____   Rating: ☆ ☆ ☆ ☆ ☆

○ Walking ○ Sit ○ Down ○ Look ○ Touch ○ Place ○ Other

Repetitions: _____   Successful: _____

Notes:

Behaviours observed today (ABC's):

Week Two

What went well, and how I can improve:

Weekly Rating: ☆ ☆ ☆ ☆ ☆

Habit Tracker: Habits (good and bad) that you worked on this week:

Habits	M	T	W	T	F	S	S
	○	○	○	○	○	○	○
	○	○	○	○	○	○	○
	○	○	○	○	○	○	○

Expert Tip #2

Barking

Management

- Do not yell at the dog when they are barking.

- Minimise exposure to the stimuli to prevent rehearsal of the behaviour.

- Where boredom is a factor ensure the dog's needs for exercise and enrichment are met prior to extended periods of absence. Consider the use of puzzle toys, kongs or the use of a dog walking service, or doggy day care.

- Consider the use of window film, curtains, baby gates etc. to limit access to triggers.

- Consider the use of television or radio during periods of absence to limit the intensity of evocative stimuli.

Differential Reinforcement of Other (DRO) Behaviours

- Condition the Clicker, or Marker Word "Yes!".

- Condition "Look" and "Touch" cues.

- Expose the dog to the trigger - mark and reward the dog for doing anything other than barking, this may be attending to you, look, touch, or just remaining calm.

- Increase the intensity of the trigger slowly and repeat.

Tips for Long-Term Success

- Be consistent—every family member and visitor should follow the same rules.

- Avoid yelling at the dog, as this can be seen as you joining in barking.

- Use high-value treats to reinforce calm behaviour in high-arousal situations.

By understanding the **ABC's of Dog Behaviour** and implementing these strategies, you can teach your dog not to bark at things that trigger it. Patience and consistency are key!

** Use the **Barking Record** on Pg 85

M T W T F S S Date: ___ / ___

Time: _____   Dawn Day Dusk Night   _____ °

Time spent exercising today: _____

○ Walk   ○ Hike   ○ Jog / Run   ○ Fetch   ○ Tug   ○ Swimming   ○ Sport
○ Playing with other dogs   ○ Other _____

Notes:

Time spent training today: _____   Rating: ☆ ☆ ☆ ☆ ☆

○ Walking   ○ Sit   ○ Down   ○ Look   ○ Touch   ○ Place   ○ Other

Repetitions: _____   Successful: _____

Notes:

Behaviours observed today (ABC's):

Doggy Diary - Behaviour Edition

M T W T F S S   Date: ___ / ___

Time: _____   Dawn Day Dusk Night   _____ °

Time spent exercising today: _____

○ Walk   ○ Hike   ○ Jog / Run   ○ Fetch   ○ Tug   ○ Swimming   ○ Sport
○ Playing with other dogs   ○ Other _____

Notes:

Time spent training today: _____   Rating: ☆ ☆ ☆ ☆ ☆

○ Walking   ○ Sit   ○ Down   ○ Look   ○ Touch   ○ Place   ○ Other

Repetitions: _____   Successful: _____

Notes:

Behaviours observed today (ABC's):

M T W T F S S   Date: ___ / ___

Time: _____   Dawn Day Dusk Night   _____ °

Time spent exercising today: _____

○ Walk   ○ Hike   ○ Jog / Run   ○ Fetch   ○ Tug   ○ Swimming   ○ Sport
○ Playing with other dogs   ○ Other _____

Notes:

Time spent training today: _____   Rating: ☆ ☆ ☆ ☆ ☆

○ Walking   ○ Sit   ○ Down   ○ Look   ○ Touch   ○ Place   ○ Other

Repetitions: _____   Successful: _____

Notes:

Behaviours observed today (ABC's):

M T W T F S S   Date: __ / __

Time: _____   Dawn Day Dusk Night   _____ °

Time spent exercising today: _____

○ Walk ○ Hike ○ Jog / Run ○ Fetch ○ Tug ○ Swimming ○ Sport
○ Playing with other dogs ○ Other _____

Notes:

Time spent training today: _____   Rating: ☆ ☆ ☆ ☆ ☆

○ Walking ○ Sit ○ Down ○ Look ○ Touch ○ Place ○ Other

Repetitions: _____   Successful: _____

Notes:

Behaviours observed today (ABC's):

M T W T F S S   Date: ___ / ___

Time: _____   Dawn Day Dusk Night   _____ °

Time spent exercising today: _____

○ Walk ○ Hike ○ Jog / Run ○ Fetch ○ Tug ○ Swimming ○ Sport
○ Playing with other dogs ○ Other _____

Notes:

Time spent training today: _____   Rating: ☆ ☆ ☆ ☆ ☆

○ Walking ○ Sit ○ Down ○ Look ○ Touch ○ Place ○ Other

Repetitions: _____   Successful: _____

Notes:

Behaviours observed today (ABC's):

M T W T F S S   Date: ___ / ___

Time: _____   Dawn Day Dusk Night   _____ °

Time spent exercising today: _____

○ Walk ○ Hike ○ Jog / Run ○ Fetch ○ Tug ○ Swimming ○ Sport
○ Playing with other dogs ○ Other _____

Notes:

Time spent training today: _____   Rating: ☆ ☆ ☆ ☆ ☆

○ Walking ○ Sit ○ Down ○ Look ○ Touch ○ Place ○ Other

Repetitions: _____   Successful: _____

Notes:

Behaviours observed today (ABC's):

Doggy Diary - Behaviour Edition

M T W T F S S Date: ___ / ___

Time: _____   Dawn Day Dusk Night   ____ °

Time spent exercising today: _____

○ Walk ○ Hike ○ Jog / Run ○ Fetch ○ Tug ○ Swimming ○ Sport
○ Playing with other dogs ○ Other _____

Notes:

Time spent training today: _____   Rating: ☆ ☆ ☆ ☆ ☆

○ Walking ○ Sit ○ Down ○ Look ○ Touch ○ Place ○ Other

Repetitions: _____ Successful: _____

Notes:

Behaviours observed today (ABC's):

Week Three

What went well, and how I can improve:

Weekly Rating: ☆ ☆ ☆ ☆ ☆

Habit Tracker: Habits (good and bad) that you worked on this week:

Habits	M	T	W	T	F	S	S
	○	○	○	○	○	○	○
	○	○	○	○	○	○	○
	○	○	○	○	○	○	○

Expert Tip #3

Fears & Phobias

Management

- Fear is a natural response to real or perceived threats, whereas a phobia is an excessive and irrational fear.

- Your dog could be fearful of other dogs or strangers or have a phobia about the wheelie bin.

- Fears and phobias often start during the fear periods, the first being 8 to 12 weeks, and the second being 6 to 12 months.

- Limit uncontrolled exposure to the aversive stimulus.

- Don't force your dog to confront the stimulus at full intensity.

- Avoid trying to calm your dog by patting and saying "Good Dog" as this can reinforce fearful behaviour.

- Do use constant pressure - with a Thundershirt, or by your body.

Build Confidence

- Fearful dogs lack confidence, so our aim is to build confidence in the situations that evoke fear.

- Condition the Clicker, or Marker Word "Yes!".

- Condition "Sit", "Stand", "Down", "Look", and "Touch" cues.

- Train every day at regular times for short intervals, 5-10 minutes is plenty.

- Condition your dog to play with a good game of fetch and/or tug.

- Walk regularly and incorporate some play into your walks.

- Look for things in the environment for the dog to climb on and interact with, different surfaces, fallen logs, water, chairs and tables, kids play equipment. Encourage but do not force your dog.

- There are several ways to use kiddies clam shell pools:
    - Fill up the pool with empty plastic bottles or ball pit balls. Start with just a few and add more as your dog gets more confident. Throw the dogs food, or a high value treat into the pool. The dog must jump into the pool to search for the food or treat.
    - Put their ball in the pool with an inch of water in it. Slowly increase the depth.
    - Fill the pool with play sand and bury a Kong - slowly bury the Kong deeper.

Desensitise Through Controlled Exposure

- Control the environment so that your dog is exposed to the stimulus and a very low level.

- Example: If your dog is fearful of noise start at low volume, if your dog is afraid of inanimate objects start at a good distance from it.

- During the exposure you can do obedience, play with your dog, or just hang out, whichever the dog finds more comforting to begin with.

- Make the experience very rewarding for your dog, use lots of praise, pats and high value treats.

- Slowly increased the intensity of the stimulus.

- Over time offer less interaction and reward the dog for paying attention to you when they are exposed to the stimulus.

- Depending on the severity of the fear or phobia this may take months, or years of training.

- Anti-anxiety medication may be useful in severe cases, but only with a behaviour modification plan.

M T W T F S S Date: ___ / ___

Time: _____   Dawn Day Dusk Night   _____ °

Time spent exercising today: _____

○ Walk ○ Hike ○ Jog / Run ○ Fetch ○ Tug ○ Swimming ○ Sport
○ Playing with other dogs ○ Other _____

Notes:

Time spent training today: _____   Rating: ☆ ☆ ☆ ☆ ☆

○ Walking ○ Sit ○ Down ○ Look ○ Touch ○ Place ○ Other

Repetitions: _____   Successful: _____

Notes:

Behaviours observed today (ABC's):

M T W T F S S Date: ___ / ___

Time: _____   Dawn Day Dusk Night   _____ °

Time spent exercising today: _____

○ Walk ○ Hike ○ Jog / Run ○ Fetch ○ Tug ○ Swimming ○ Sport
○ Playing with other dogs ○ Other _____

Notes:

Time spent training today: _____   Rating: ☆ ☆ ☆ ☆ ☆

○ Walking ○ Sit ○ Down ○ Look ○ Touch ○ Place ○ Other

Repetitions: _____   Successful: _____

Notes:

Behaviours observed today (ABC's):

M T W T F S S Date: ___ / ___

Time: _____   Dawn Day Dusk Night   _____ °

Time spent exercising today: _____

○ Walk ○ Hike ○ Jog / Run ○ Fetch ○ Tug ○ Swimming ○ Sport
○ Playing with other dogs ○ Other _____

Notes:

Time spent training today: _____   Rating: ☆ ☆ ☆ ☆ ☆

○ Walking ○ Sit ○ Down ○ Look ○ Touch ○ Place ○ Other

Repetitions: _____   Successful: _____

Notes:

Behaviours observed today (ABC's):

MTWTFSS Date: ___ / ___

Time: _____   Dawn Day Dusk Night   _____ °

Time spent exercising today: _____

○ Walk   ○ Hike   ○ Jog / Run   ○ Fetch   ○ Tug   ○ Swimming   ○ Sport
○ Playing with other dogs   ○ Other _____

Notes:

Time spent training today: _____   Rating: ☆ ☆ ☆ ☆ ☆

○ Walking   ○ Sit   ○ Down   ○ Look   ○ Touch   ○ Place   ○ Other

Repetitions: _____   Successful: _____

Notes:

Behaviours observed today (ABC's):

M T W T F S S Date: ___ / ___

Time: _____   Dawn Day Dusk Night   _____ °

Time spent exercising today: _____

○ Walk ○ Hike ○ Jog / Run ○ Fetch ○ Tug ○ Swimming ○ Sport
○ Playing with other dogs ○ Other _____

Notes:

Time spent training today: _____   Rating: ☆ ☆ ☆ ☆ ☆

○ Walking ○ Sit ○ Down ○ Look ○ Touch ○ Place ○ Other

Repetitions: _____   Successful: _____

Notes:

Behaviours observed today (ABC's):

M T W T F S S   Date: ___ / ___

Time: _____   Dawn Day Dusk Night   _____ °

Time spent exercising today: _____

○ Walk ○ Hike ○ Jog / Run ○ Fetch ○ Tug ○ Swimming ○ Sport
○ Playing with other dogs ○ Other _____

Notes:

Time spent training today: _____   Rating: ☆ ☆ ☆ ☆ ☆

○ Walking ○ Sit ○ Down ○ Look ○ Touch ○ Place ○ Other

Repetitions: _____   Successful: _____

Notes:

Behaviours observed today (ABC's):

M T W T F S S   Date: ___ / ___

Time: _____   Dawn Day Dusk Night   _____ °

Time spent exercising today: _____

○ Walk ○ Hike ○ Jog / Run ○ Fetch ○ Tug ○ Swimming ○ Sport
○ Playing with other dogs ○ Other _____

Notes:

Time spent training today: _____   Rating: ☆ ☆ ☆ ☆ ☆

○ Walking ○ Sit ○ Down ○ Look ○ Touch ○ Place ○ Other

Repetitions: _____   Successful: _____

Notes:

Behaviours observed today (ABC's):

Week Four

What went well, and how I can improve:

Weekly Rating: ☆ ☆ ☆ ☆ ☆

Habit Tracker: Habits (good and bad) that you worked on this week:

Habits	M	T	W	T	F	S	S
	○	○	○	○	○	○	○
	○	○	○	○	○	○	○
	○	○	○	○	○	○	○

Expert Tip #4

Separation Anxiety

Management

- Separation anxiety (SA) is a disorder in which the dog experiences excessive anxiety when away from home, or from their owner.

- SA occurs immediately on separation and is not related to how long you are gone for. If time is a factor the more likely diagnosis is boredom.

- SA manifests as nuisance barking, chewing, digging, toileting or destructive behaviour.

- Don't make a big fuss when you leave, or when you return.

- Ensure the dog's needs for exercise and enrichment are met prior to extended periods of absence.

- Consider the use of television or radio for background noise when your absent.

- Consider the use of puzzle toys, kongs or the use of a dog walking service, or doggy day care.

Desensitise Pre-Departure Routine

- Make a list of all pre-departure activities that trigger your dog. This could include:

    o Getting dressed for work.

    o Picking up your bag or car keys.

    o Taking a shower.

    o Doing your hair & makeup.

The aim here is to de-couple each activity with the act of leaving the house.

Work through the list by doing them one at a time without leaving the house.

Example: Pick up your car keys and then sit down to watch tv.

- Once your dog does not show any anxiety when you pick up the car keys move to the next thing on the list.

- Depending on how severe the SA is, and how long the list is, you can expect this to take several months.

Counter Condition Gradual Absences

- Condition the Clicker, or Marker Word "Yes!".

- Condition "Place" on a comfy dog bed.

- Have your dog place while you walk into the next room.

- Have your dog place and practice some of the pre-departure activities without leaving.

- Have your dog place and leave the house, but not by the front door.

- Finally have your dog place and leave the house via the front door.

- In each of these steps slowly increase the duration of your absence, starting at a few seconds, until the dog can remain calm for a few minutes.

- Always return to the dog on place to reward and remain calm.

- At this stage start putting down a Kong filled with high value treats before you leave.

Expert Tips for Long-Term Success

- Be consistent—every family member and visitor should follow the same rules.

- Use high-value treats to reinforce calm behaviour in high-arousal situations.

M T W T F S S   Date: ___ / ___

Time: _____   Dawn Day Dusk Night   _____ °

Time spent exercising today: _____

○ Walk ○ Hike ○ Jog / Run ○ Fetch ○ Tug ○ Swimming ○ Sport
○ Playing with other dogs ○ Other _____

Notes:

Time spent training today: _____   Rating: ☆ ☆ ☆ ☆ ☆

○ Walking ○ Sit ○ Down ○ Look ○ Touch ○ Place ○ Other

Repetitions: _____   Successful: _____

Notes:

Behaviours observed today (ABC's):

Doggy Diary - Behaviour Edition

M T W T F S S Date: __ / __

Time: _____   Dawn Day Dusk Night   _____ °

Time spent exercising today: _____

○ Walk ○ Hike ○ Jog / Run ○ Fetch ○ Tug ○ Swimming ○ Sport
○ Playing with other dogs ○ Other _____

Notes:

Time spent training today: _____   Rating: ☆ ☆ ☆ ☆ ☆

○ Walking ○ Sit ○ Down ○ Look ○ Touch ○ Place ○ Other

Repetitions: _____   Successful: _____

Notes:

Behaviours observed today (ABC's):

M T W T F S S   Date: ___ / ___

Time: _____   Dawn Day Dusk Night   _____ °

Time spent exercising today: _____

○ Walk ○ Hike ○ Jog / Run ○ Fetch ○ Tug ○ Swimming ○ Sport
○ Playing with other dogs ○ Other _____

Notes:

Time spent training today: _____   Rating: ☆ ☆ ☆ ☆ ☆

○ Walking ○ Sit ○ Down ○ Look ○ Touch ○ Place ○ Other

Repetitions: _____   Successful: _____

Notes:

Behaviours observed today (ABC's):

M T W T F S S Date: ___ / ___

Time: _____   Dawn Day Dusk Night   _____ °

Time spent exercising today: _____

○ Walk ○ Hike ○ Jog / Run ○ Fetch ○ Tug ○ Swimming ○ Sport
○ Playing with other dogs ○ Other _____

Notes:

Time spent training today: _____   Rating: ☆ ☆ ☆ ☆ ☆

○ Walking ○ Sit ○ Down ○ Look ○ Touch ○ Place ○ Other

Repetitions: _____   Successful: _____

Notes:

Behaviours observed today (ABC's):

Doggy Diary - Behaviour Edition

M T W T F S S Date: ___ / ___

Time: _____   Dawn Day Dusk Night   _____ °

Time spent exercising today: _____

○ Walk ○ Hike ○ Jog / Run ○ Fetch ○ Tug ○ Swimming ○ Sport
○ Playing with other dogs ○ Other _____

Notes:

Time spent training today: _____   Rating: ☆ ☆ ☆ ☆ ☆

○ Walking ○ Sit ○ Down ○ Look ○ Touch ○ Place ○ Other

Repetitions: _____   Successful: _____

Notes:

Behaviours observed today (ABC's):

Doggy Diary - Behaviour Edition

M T W T F S S   Date: ___ / ___

Time: _____   Dawn Day Dusk Night   _____ o

Time spent exercising today: _____

○ Walk ○ Hike ○ Jog / Run ○ Fetch ○ Tug ○ Swimming ○ Sport
○ Playing with other dogs ○ Other _____

Notes:

Time spent training today: _____   Rating: ☆ ☆ ☆ ☆ ☆

○ Walking ○ Sit ○ Down ○ Look ○ Touch ○ Place ○ Other

Repetitions: _____   Successful: _____

Notes:

Behaviours observed today (ABC's):

Doggy Diary - Behaviour Edition

M T W T F S S Date: ___ / ___

Time: _____   Dawn Day Dusk Night   _____ °

Time spent exercising today: _____

○ Walk ○ Hike ○ Jog / Run ○ Fetch ○ Tug ○ Swimming ○ Sport
○ Playing with other dogs ○ Other _____

Notes:

Time spent training today: _____   Rating: ☆ ☆ ☆ ☆ ☆

○ Walking ○ Sit ○ Down ○ Look ○ Touch ○ Place ○ Other

Repetitions: _____   Successful: _____

Notes:

Behaviours observed today (ABC's):

Week Five

What went well, and how I can improve:

Weekly Rating: ☆ ☆ ☆ ☆ ☆

Habit Tracker: Habits (good and bad) that you worked on this week:

Habits	M	T	W	T	F	S	S
	○	○	○	○	○	○	○
	○	○	○	○	○	○	○
	○	○	○	○	○	○	○

Expert Tip #5

Loose Leash Walking

Door Manners

The walk starts as soon as you connect the leash, so start your dog in the right mindset with good door manners. Condition the dog to 'Sit' and 'Wait' as the door is opened before being cued to exit with 'Okay' or 'Let's go'. Use the opening and closing of the door to reinforce this behaviour. Sitting gets the door open, breaking the sit gets the door closed.

Leash Pressure

If you are going to use a collar or slip lead you MUST teach the dog how to respond to leash pressure. This is done by applying gentle and consistent pressure at a level horizontal to the ground at the same height as the collar. Don't say anything when applying pressure. When the dog yields to the pressure and attends to you mark and treat. Shuffle backwards as their head turns and make it fun!

Auto Sit

Train the dog to automatically sit every time you stop. At the beginning take one step (if your dog already pulls take half a step) then cue them into a sit and treat. Progress to a whole step, then two, then three. In time the dog will anticipate the stop and sit so pulling on the leash becomes less intense.

Direction Changes

Regularly changing direction during walking conditions the dog to pay closer attention to your movements. These can be anywhere from 45° to 180°. A U-Turn is particularly helpful for a dog that urges ahead, a few sharp U-Turns will quickly condition the dog to pay closer attention to their position relative to you.

Checking In

When the dog looks up at you mark and reward. You can use the clicker or mark with 'Yes!'. Watch for this when you make turns. If it doesn't happen very often cue it by talking to your dog.

M T W T F S S Date: ___ / ___

Time: _____   Dawn Day Dusk Night   _____ °

Time spent exercising today: _____

○ Walk   ○ Hike   ○ Jog / Run   ○ Fetch   ○ Tug   ○ Swimming   ○ Sport
○ Playing with other dogs   ○ Other _____

Notes:

Time spent training today: _____   Rating: ☆ ☆ ☆ ☆ ☆

○ Walking   ○ Sit   ○ Down   ○ Look   ○ Touch   ○ Place   ○ Other

Repetitions: _____   Successful: _____

Notes:

Behaviours observed today (ABC's):

M T W T F S S   Date: ___ / ___

Time: _____   Dawn Day Dusk Night   _____ °

Time spent exercising today: _____

○ Walk   ○ Hike   ○ Jog / Run   ○ Fetch   ○ Tug   ○ Swimming   ○ Sport
○ Playing with other dogs   ○ Other _____

Notes:

Time spent training today: _____   Rating: ☆ ☆ ☆ ☆ ☆

○ Walking   ○ Sit   ○ Down   ○ Look   ○ Touch   ○ Place   ○ Other

Repetitions: _____   Successful: _____

Notes:

Behaviours observed today (ABC's):

M T W T F S S   Date: ___ / ___

Time: _____   Dawn Day Dusk Night   _____ °

Time spent exercising today: _____

○ Walk ○ Hike ○ Jog / Run ○ Fetch ○ Tug ○ Swimming ○ Sport
○ Playing with other dogs ○ Other _____

Notes:

Time spent training today: _____   Rating: ☆ ☆ ☆ ☆ ☆

○ Walking ○ Sit ○ Down ○ Look ○ Touch ○ Place ○ Other

Repetitions: _____   Successful: _____

Notes:

Behaviours observed today (ABC's):

M T W T F S S Date: ___ / ___

Time: _____   Dawn Day Dusk Night   _____ °

Time spent exercising today: _____

○ Walk ○ Hike ○ Jog / Run ○ Fetch ○ Tug ○ Swimming ○ Sport
○ Playing with other dogs ○ Other _____

Notes:

Time spent training today: _____   Rating: ☆ ☆ ☆ ☆ ☆

○ Walking ○ Sit ○ Down ○ Look ○ Touch ○ Place ○ Other

Repetitions: _____   Successful: _____

Notes:

Behaviours observed today (ABC's):

M T W T F S S Date: ___ / ___

Time: _____   Dawn Day Dusk Night   _____ °

Time spent exercising today: _____

○ Walk ○ Hike ○ Jog / Run ○ Fetch ○ Tug ○ Swimming ○ Sport
○ Playing with other dogs ○ Other _____

Notes:

Time spent training today: _____   Rating: ☆ ☆ ☆ ☆ ☆

○ Walking ○ Sit ○ Down ○ Look ○ Touch ○ Place ○ Other

Repetitions: _____   Successful: _____

Notes:

Behaviours observed today (ABC's):

Doggy Diary - Behaviour Edition

M T W T F S S Date: ___ / ___

Time: _____   Dawn Day Dusk Night   _____ °

Time spent exercising today: _____

○ Walk ○ Hike ○ Jog / Run ○ Fetch ○ Tug ○ Swimming ○ Sport
○ Playing with other dogs ○ Other _____

Notes:

Time spent training today: _____   Rating: ☆ ☆ ☆ ☆ ☆

○ Walking ○ Sit ○ Down ○ Look ○ Touch ○ Place ○ Other

Repetitions: _____   Successful: _____

Notes:

Behaviours observed today (ABC's):

M T W T F S S   Date: ___ / ___

Time: _____   Dawn Day Dusk Night   _____ °

Time spent exercising today: _____

○ Walk ○ Hike ○ Jog / Run ○ Fetch ○ Tug ○ Swimming ○ Sport
○ Playing with other dogs ○ Other _____

Notes:

Time spent training today: _____   Rating: ☆ ☆ ☆ ☆ ☆

○ Walking ○ Sit ○ Down ○ Look ○ Touch ○ Place ○ Other

Repetitions: _____   Successful: _____

Notes:

Behaviours observed today (ABC's):

Week Six

What went well, and how I can improve: Weekly Rating: ☆ ☆ ☆ ☆ ☆

Habit Tracker: Habits (good and bad) that you worked on this week:

Habits	M	T	W	T	F	S	S
	○	○	○	○	○	○	○
	○	○	○	○	○	○	○
	○	○	○	○	○	○	○

Expert Tip #6

Leash & Tethering

The Leash isn't just for outside...

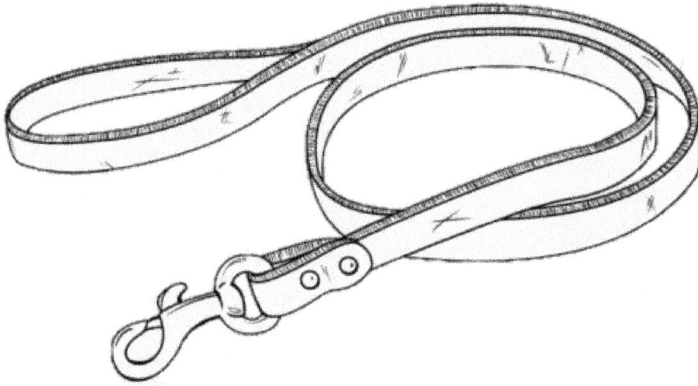

It's for when you need more control!

When to use:

- Limit Jumping up.
- Reduce Barking for attention.
- Control Alert barking at the front door.
- Minimise Chewing on furniture.
- Prevent Counter surfing.
- Tether to reinforce place command & promote relaxation.

M T W T F S S   Date: ___ / ___

Time: _____   Dawn Day Dusk Night   _____ °

Time spent exercising today: _____

○ Walk ○ Hike ○ Jog / Run ○ Fetch ○ Tug ○ Swimming ○ Sport
○ Playing with other dogs ○ Other _____

Notes:

Time spent training today: _____   Rating: ☆ ☆ ☆ ☆ ☆

○ Walking ○ Sit ○ Down ○ Look ○ Touch ○ Place ○ Other

Repetitions: _____   Successful: _____

Notes:

Behaviours observed today (ABC's):

M T W T F S S   Date: ___ / ___

Time: _____   Dawn Day Dusk Night   _____ °

Time spent exercising today: _____

○ Walk ○ Hike ○ Jog / Run ○ Fetch ○ Tug ○ Swimming ○ Sport
○ Playing with other dogs ○ Other _____

Notes:

Time spent training today: _____   Rating: ☆ ☆ ☆ ☆ ☆

○ Walking ○ Sit ○ Down ○ Look ○ Touch ○ Place ○ Other

Repetitions: _____   Successful: _____

Notes:

Behaviours observed today (ABC's):

Doggy Diary - Behaviour Edition

M T W T F S S   Date: ___ / ___

Time: _____   Dawn Day Dusk Night   _____ °

Time spent exercising today: _____

○ Walk ○ Hike ○ Jog / Run ○ Fetch ○ Tug ○ Swimming ○ Sport
○ Playing with other dogs ○ Other _____

Notes:

Time spent training today: _____   Rating: ☆ ☆ ☆ ☆ ☆

○ Walking ○ Sit ○ Down ○ Look ○ Touch ○ Place ○ Other

Repetitions: _____   Successful: _____

Notes:

Behaviours observed today (ABC's):

MTWTFSS Date: ___ / ___

Time: _____   Dawn Day Dusk Night   _____ °

Time spent exercising today: _____

○ Walk ○ Hike ○ Jog / Run ○ Fetch ○ Tug ○ Swimming ○ Sport
○ Playing with other dogs ○ Other _____

Notes:

Time spent training today: _____   Rating: ☆ ☆ ☆ ☆ ☆

○ Walking ○ Sit ○ Down ○ Look ○ Touch ○ Place ○ Other

Repetitions: _____   Successful: _____

Notes:

Behaviours observed today (ABC's):

M T W T F S S Date: ___ / ___

Time: _____   Dawn Day Dusk Night   _____ °

Time spent exercising today: _____

O Walk O Hike O Jog / Run O Fetch O Tug O Swimming O Sport
O Playing with other dogs O Other _____

Notes:

Time spent training today: _____   Rating: ☆ ☆ ☆ ☆ ☆

O Walking O Sit O Down O Look O Touch O Place O Other

Repetitions: _____   Successful: _____

Notes:

Behaviours observed today (ABC's):

M T W T F S S   Date: ___ / ___

Time: _____   Dawn Day Dusk Night   ____ °

Time spent exercising today: _____

○ Walk ○ Hike ○ Jog / Run ○ Fetch ○ Tug ○ Swimming ○ Sport
○ Playing with other dogs ○ Other _____

Notes:

Time spent training today: _____   Rating: ☆ ☆ ☆ ☆ ☆

○ Walking ○ Sit ○ Down ○ Look ○ Touch ○ Place ○ Other

Repetitions: _____   Successful: _____

Notes:

Behaviours observed today (ABC's):

M T W T F S S Date: ___ / ___

Time: _____   Dawn Day Dusk Night   _____ °

Time spent exercising today: _____

O Walk O Hike O Jog / Run O Fetch O Tug O Swimming O Sport
O Playing with other dogs O Other _____

Notes:

Time spent training today: _____   Rating: ★ ★ ★ ★ ★

O Walking O Sit O Down O Look O Touch O Place O Other

Repetitions: _____   Successful: _____

Notes:

Behaviours observed today (ABC's):

Week Seven

What went well, and how I can improve:

Weekly Rating: ☆ ☆ ☆ ☆ ☆

Habit Tracker: Habits (good and bad) that you worked on this week:

Habits	M	T	W	T	F	S	S
	○	○	○	○	○	○	○
	○	○	○	○	○	○	○
	○	○	○	○	○	○	○

Leave the TV or Radio on when you're not home.

When to use

- Can relieve boredom and reduce stress during absences.

- Start with a low volume and choose relaxing classical music.

- YouTube has dog relaxation music that plays for 12 hours.

- Makes it normal for the dog - the house can be very quiet without you

- Masks outside noises made by neighbours and other dogs.

M T W T F S S Date: ___ / ___

Time: _____   Dawn Day Dusk Night   _____ °

Time spent exercising today: _____

○ Walk ○ Hike ○ Jog / Run ○ Fetch ○ Tug ○ Swimming ○ Sport
○ Playing with other dogs ○ Other _____

Notes:

Time spent training today: _____   Rating: ☆ ☆ ☆ ☆ ☆

○ Walking ○ Sit ○ Down ○ Look ○ Touch ○ Place ○ Other

Repetitions: _____   Successful: _____

Notes:

Behaviours observed today (ABC's):

M T W T F S S Date: ___ / ___

Time: _____   Dawn Day Dusk Night   _____ °

Time spent exercising today: _____

○ Walk ○ Hike ○ Jog / Run ○ Fetch ○ Tug ○ Swimming ○ Sport
○ Playing with other dogs ○ Other _____

Notes:

Time spent training today: _____   Rating: ☆ ☆ ☆ ☆ ☆

○ Walking ○ Sit ○ Down ○ Look ○ Touch ○ Place ○ Other

Repetitions: _____   Successful: _____

Notes:

Behaviours observed today (ABC's):

Doggy Diary - Behaviour Edition

M T W T F S S   Date: ___ / ___

Time: _____   Dawn Day Dusk Night   _____ °

Time spent exercising today: _____

○ Walk ○ Hike ○ Jog / Run ○ Fetch ○ Tug ○ Swimming ○ Sport
○ Playing with other dogs ○ Other _____

Notes:

Time spent training today: _____   Rating: ☆ ☆ ☆ ☆ ☆

○ Walking ○ Sit ○ Down ○ Look ○ Touch ○ Place ○ Other

Repetitions: _____   Successful: _____

Notes:

Behaviours observed today (ABC's):

Doggy Diary - Behaviour Edition

M T W T F S S   Date: ___ / ___

Time: _____   Dawn   Day   Dusk   Night   _____ °

Time spent exercising today: _____

○ Walk   ○ Hike   ○ Jog / Run   ○ Fetch   ○ Tug   ○ Swimming   ○ Sport
○ Playing with other dogs   ○ Other _____

Notes:

Time spent training today: _____   Rating: ☆ ☆ ☆ ☆ ☆

○ Walking   ○ Sit   ○ Down   ○ Look   ○ Touch   ○ Place   ○ Other

Repetitions: _____   Successful: _____

Notes:

Behaviours observed today (ABC's):

M T W T F S S   Date: __ / __

Time: _____   Dawn Day Dusk Night   _____ °

Time spent exercising today: _____

○ Walk   ○ Hike   ○ Jog / Run   ○ Fetch   ○ Tug   ○ Swimming   ○ Sport
○ Playing with other dogs   ○ Other _____

Notes:

Time spent training today: _____   Rating: ☆ ☆ ☆ ☆ ☆

○ Walking   ○ Sit   ○ Down   ○ Look   ○ Touch   ○ Place   ○ Other

Repetitions: _____   Successful: _____

Notes:

Behaviours observed today (ABC's):

Doggy Diary - Behaviour Edition

M T W T F S S   Date: ___ / ___

Time: _____   Dawn Day Dusk Night   _____ °

Time spent exercising today: _____

○ Walk ○ Hike ○ Jog / Run ○ Fetch ○ Tug ○ Swimming ○ Sport
○ Playing with other dogs ○ Other _____

Notes:

Time spent training today: _____   Rating: ☆ ☆ ☆ ☆ ☆

○ Walking ○ Sit ○ Down ○ Look ○ Touch ○ Place ○ Other

Repetitions: _____   Successful: _____

Notes:

Behaviours observed today (ABC's):

M T W T F S S   Date: ___ / ___

Time: _____   Dawn Day Dusk Night   _____ °

Time spent exercising today: _____

○ Walk   ○ Hike   ○ Jog / Run   ○ Fetch   ○ Tug   ○ Swimming   ○ Sport
○ Playing with other dogs   ○ Other _____

Notes:

Time spent training today: _____   Rating: ✧ ✧ ✧ ✧ ✧

○ Walking   ○ Sit   ○ Down   ○ Look   ○ Touch   ○ Place   ○ Other

Repetitions: _____   Successful: _____

Notes:

Behaviours observed today (ABC's):

Week Eight

What went well, and how I can improve: Weekly Rating: ☆ ☆ ☆ ☆ ☆

Habit Tracker: Habits (good and bad) that you worked on this week:

Habits	M	T	W	T	F	S	S
	○	○	○	○	○	○	○
	○	○	○	○	○	○	○
	○	○	○	○	○	○	○

Expert Tip #8

Advice for New Pawents

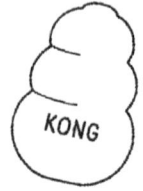

KONG

Advice for keeping your puppy happy & healthy.

Establish Routine Early: Dogs thrive on consistency. Set regular times for feeding, walks, training, and bedtime. A predictable routine reduces anxiety and helps your dog feel secure.

Prioritise Socialisation: Expose your dog to a variety of people, dogs, environments, and experiences while they are young (or gradually if adopted as an adult). Proper socialisation builds confidence and prevents fear-based behaviour later.

Focus on Positive Reinforcement: Reward good behaviour with treats, praise, or play. Avoid harsh punishment, as it can damage trust and increase fear or aggression. Reinforcing what you do want is far more effective.

Invest in Training: Teach essential cues like sit, stay, come, leave it, and loose leash walking. Even short daily training sessions (5–10 minutes) can make a big difference in obedience and safety.

Exercise and Mental Stimulation: All dogs need both physical activity and enrichment. Regular walks, play sessions, puzzle feeders, and sniffing opportunities keep them healthy and prevent boredom-related behaviours like chewing or digging.

Provide a Safe Space: Set up a quiet, comfortable area (like a crate or bed in a low-traffic room) where your dog can retreat and feel safe. This helps with rest, training, and managing stress.

Be Patient and Realistic: Training and bonding take time. Expect mistakes, especially with puppies. Stay consistent, patient, and remember progress often comes in small steps.

Barking Diary

If your dog is barking it can be helpful to make a record of how often, for how long, and how many times the dog barks, as well as what triggers it!

Date	Time Start	Time Finish	# Barks	Reason
10/4/25	0800	0815	10	Left for work

www.ingramcontent.com/pod-product-compliance
Lightning Source LLC
Chambersburg PA
CBHW071905090426
42811CB00004B/748